Island Images

Pictures of the Past from the Archives of the

Jersey Evening Post

Breedon Books
Publishing Company
Derby

First published in Great Britain by
The Breedon Books Publishing Company Limited
Breedon House, 44 Friar Gate, Derby, DE1 1DA.
1998

ISBN 1 85983 136 2

Printed and bound by Butler & Tanner Ltd., Selwood Printing Works,
Caxton Road, Frome, Somerset.

Colour separations by Freelance Repro, Leicester.

Jackets printed by Lawrence-Allen, Avon.

Contents

Foreword

7

Country Life

10

The Sea

26

People

42

At Work

54

At Play

66

Places

94

Transport

126

Royal Visitors

149

Foreword

IT is a popular myth that newspapers represent only instant disposability. While that may be true in the sense that newspaper production is an endless cycle of new editions, each one rapidly superseding the last, it is a view which ignores the existence of another, priceless asset.

As members of the media's senior service, many newspapers — the *Jersey Evening Post* among them — have been in the business long enough to have built up matchless picture archives, recording events great and small in the daily lives of the communities they serve.

The *Jersey Evening Post's* photographic treasure trove has been built up throughout the century which is now drawing to a close and its thousands of images freeze Jersey history for the enlightenment of future generations in scenes which — commonplace enough when captured — gain more impact and poignancy with each passing year. In particular, many of the pictures in this second volume bring vividly back to life the country ways and agricultural traditions of old which contributed so much to shaping our Island's very special character.

It is a pleasure to share this new selection from our unique daily record of a unique place.

Chris Bright,
Editor,
Jersey Evening Post

Country Life

Solving the problem of who looks after the kids when there is work to be done in the fields. A scene in Trinity in April 1950.

A small patch of potatoes planted by fisherman out on the Ecréhous Reef in 1936. Presumably it saved them having to go back to the Island to make fish and chips!

A rare and exciting event, the birth of triplets to a Jersey cow. Empioneeress Design, a heifer, produced them in 1949 and afterwards in 305 days recorded 10,100 lbs of milk and 505 lbs of butter-fat.

Joe Le Marquand leads his horse Bobby up the slip at La Pulente with a cart full of vraic in the early 1960s.

This calf, being shipped abroad in 1956 to join a herd in another part of the world, travelled in style to the airport by Jaguar!

Two sets of Jersey twins born at the same time on the same farm in June 1954. G.Baudains, the farmer (in the hat), Mrs Baudains, Colin Sutton of La Motte Garages, and EP reporter Jack Worboys hold the calves, while young master Baudains (right) holds one of the cows.

Hay comes in massive rolls today, but back in the post-war years it was baled and stacked like giant building blocks.

When it was planting time the whole family turned out — even the dog! This is Edouard Alexandre's farm at Sea View, L'Etacq, in 1955. He is the one holding the plough.

Children from St Martin's School were issued with jam-jars to search the beaches for Colorado beetles, the most dreaded of all threats to the Jersey Royal potato, in June 1950.

The hustle and bustle of the Weighbridge area, with masted sailing vessels in the harbour around the turn of the century.

A sight to delight any gourmet: Baskets of freshly-dug Jersey Royals — surely the finest potatoes in the world — being displayed by three French girls, Ginette, Thérèse and another Thérèse, in June 1955.

Planting spuds by hand on the slopes above L'Etacq in 1958…

…and unloading them on the docks for export back in 1950.

Vraicing in St Ouen's Bay in the days when this seaweed was considered to be one of the best — as well as the cheapest! — fertilizers in the world.

A splendid hay cart which certainly makes the most of the space above the horse.

A farmer leads his horse and load of barrelled potatoes away from the Weighbridge towards the docks during the potato season of 1937.

An unusual photograph for Jersey of the only sheep in the Island in the 1950s — despite the fact that the Island gave its name to a woollen garment.

This odd mechanism is used to stop certain heifers from continuing the bad habit of trying to suckle other heifers in their peer group.

Mountains of Jersey cider apples at John Dorey's Cider Factory at Brook Farm, St John, in the first decade of the century.

These were the days when the Jersey Royals were the most sought after potato in Britain, and potato lorries packed the St Helier Harbour area waiting to be shipped to the mainland.

It is difficult to see what this carter from F.W.Laurens, of St Helier, is loading on the quayside in 1936, but at least the horse appears to be enjoying the rest.

A serene picture of ploughing taken in 1970 beneath the old mill in St Ouen. Note the seagulls following the plough.

Best cow in show — belonging to Colin Richardson — at Springfield. The year is not known.

Hand-digging Jersey Royals in 1935 — with the toddler brought along for safe keeping.

Horse-drawn carts wait patiently for their barrels.

Potato lorries and vans in the early 1920s queue up along the Esplanade waiting to have their loads weighed on the Bridge.

Members of the local farming community gather at a farm and cattle sale held at Les Câteaux, Trinity in 1936.

These prize cattle are heading home to St. Peter after the Royal Jersey Agricultural and Horticultural Society show held at Springfield in 1938.

Jersey Royal potatoes being loaded on to the cargo ship *Josephine* for export to the UK in the 1960s. Note that by now potatoes were shipped out in sacks rather than barrels.

Pictured in 1951, outside the offices of potato exporter John Terry is 70 year old Frankie Laurens who regularly brought his potatoes to market by horse and van.

Vraic gathering at La Saline in St Ouen's Bay in 1938, was an annual activity that involved farm workers of all ages.

These farmers take a welcome break from the hectic goings-on at the St John and St Lawrence agricultural societies' spring show, held at H.P. Vibert's farm, Midland, St Lawrence in 1953.

In 1936 this new Ferguson tractor attracted a lot of attention as it was put through its paces at a demonstration held at Mr S. Le Gresley's farm at St. Ouen.

In 1938, well known Gorey fisherman Tom Le Huquet takes advantage of the spring sunshine and low water to calmly mend his nets.

Under the watchful eye of man's best friend, grading and bunching the Spring harvest of daffodils for the Easter market, goes on at a farm in St. Peter, in 1937.

Judging by the attire of States' Inspector Mr. J.R. Le Sueur, the early morning sunshine belies the chill in the air on the New North Quay, as he holds up a fine truss of outdoor tomatoes, in 1937.

In the days before the combine harvester hay making was a hot and strenuous task, as this 1936 scene depicts.

Members of the Jersey Young Farmers Club gathered for the camera at Rozel campsite in the autumn of 1969 to mark the club's 50th birthday.

The Sea

The tiny port of Gorey pictured from the ramparts of Mont Orgueil and showing the many private pleasure boats as well as fishing boats which use the harbour. Taken in the 1970s, this picture is timeless.

A photograph from the Victoria and Albert Museum collection entitled 'Washing the Boat, Jersey, 1893' but otherwise unidentified.

The mailboat *Caesarea* makes an impressive sight and plenty of smoke as she leaves St Helier Harbour on a spring tide in 1962. Note the height of the water against the pier-head.

The *Brockley Combe,* which sank off the Minquiers reef in December 1953 on passage from Guernsey to Jersey. She was a total loss.

A turn of the century photograph of St Helier Harbour, showing a fine mixture of steam and sail.

The States tug approaches the Minquiers reef off the south coast on an official visit in 1949.

The States tug sits among the treacherous rocks of the Minquiers while the visitors inspect the buildings on the reef.

The Union Flag flies over the cottages at the Minquiers. For many years the French have laid claim to the reef, but Jersey has loyally kept them for the Crown.

Small craft buffet and vie with each other for places during the Gorey Regatta of 1948.

This is believed to be the last trip of the mailboat *Isle of Jersey* — on 31 October 1959 — before she went to the breaker's yard.

The boat without which large ships would be unable to enter or leave St Helier Harbour — the 'No 1' pilot boat in May 1951.

The SS *Reindeer* berthed in St Helier Harbour beside the GWR offices in the early 1920s.

The mailboat *Isle of Sark* off the Jersey coast in the early 1930s…

…and the Southern Railway cruising ship the SS *St Briac* in the 1920s. Both were familiar vessels in Channel Island waters.

A Jersey fisherman and his lad in the early part of the century…

…and another making crab pots from willow.

The view into town from the New North Quay at the beginning of the century, with masted coalers at the quayside and hotels and warehouses around the Weighbridge area. Queen Victoria stands imperiously on her plinth in the centre of it all.

The dredger *Le Belon* of St Malo working on the bed of St Aubin's Harbour in April 1967.

Possibly the best-known of all Jersey ships, *La Duchesse de Normandie*, known to all, very affectionately, as *'Sooty'*, because of the voluminous clouds of smoke she emitted from her stack, pictured here in 1967…

…and her sister ship, *La Duchesse de Bretagne,* which naturally had to be christened *'Sweep',* in 1969.

The States tug *Duke of Normandy* carrying a cargo of sailors in 1932. She was the boat used when anyone left a request to be buried at sea.

One of the 'new' car ferries which usurped the old mailboats. The Channel Island Ferries' *Corbière* arrives in St Helier Harbour in March 1985.

The mailboat *Sarnia* and her sister ship *Caesarea,* lying at the Albert Pier, make an impressive sight in 1963. Both went to the breakers in 1987.

The *Jersey Star,* a 44-foot, 12-ton fishing trawler, was found holed behind Rozel Harbour in March 1960. It seems that the almost new vessel had broken away from her moorings. Here, divers are assessing the damage to her in choppy seas.

These women are ormering at low tide behind Elizabeth Castle in February 1952…

…and these lads are demonstrating for the camera what a fine catch they had two decades or so earlier.

The oldest photograph in this book. Taken in about 1851 from the top of Mont Orgueil Castle, it shows the Gorey shipyards of Fauvel, Noel, Bellot, Picot, Aubin, Cantel and Messervy.

The Humane Society's Medal is presented at the then Government Offices at La Collette to pier-heads watchman Patrick Thomas Casey for his bravery in February 1948 in saving a life in St Helier Harbour.

The *Tien Ho* broke free from her moorings in March 1972 but she was saved from being broken up on the rocks and has since been sailed across the Atlantic and back!

This picture of sailors unloading a crate marked for the Lieut-Governor was taken when mess room silver from HMS *Jersey* was returned to the Island in February 1954.

In 1939, this dartboard was made out of 30,000 matchsticks by the man holding it, a Mr Chevalier.

Mr Battle, Des O'Connor, escorted Miss Battle of Flowers, Diana Le Bot, in 1977.

At Work

A magnificent display of groceries manufactured by Coombs on display in an exhibition in the original West Park Pavilion known to all around the turn of the century as 'the Tin House'.

Members of the St Helier Paid Police march smartly through the streets of the town one misty morning in 1935. The fact that they were wearing medals suggests they were probably heading for the Armistice Day parade.

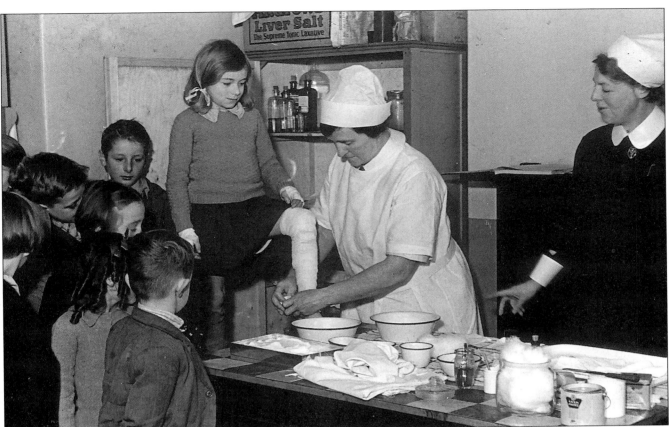

A poorly knee is bandaged by Nurse Ashworth under the watchful eye of Sister, while school friends look on, in the 1930s.

Bicycles and baskets at the ready, four district nurses pose outside the ante-natal clinic at Gloucester Lodge, Stopford Road, in 1939.

No, it's not some strange Jersey ritual, but inspectors of the Jersey New Waterworks Company checking for leaks after an exceptionally heavy load destined for the Jersey Electricity Company had passed this way in 1968.

Trying to dry out the waterlogged football pitch at Springfield in March 1980 was a monumental task. Today the buildings behind the groundsmen have been demolished, the pitch completely relaid and the stadium rebuilt.

One of Jersey's most popular holiday souvenirs — and one which is unique to the Island — is the 'long jack' or cabbage walking stick. Here the stalks, straight from the field, are being unloaded at L'Etacq Woodcrafts ready to be turned into strong smart canes.

Was it that schooldays were not the best days of one's life in the 19th century, or was it that it was obligatory to look serious in school photographs? Either way, the pupils of St Paul's in May 1897 apparently had nothing to smile about.

Every picture tells a story, and in this case two. In October 1962 the States decided that white lines should be painted on the flagstones of the Royal Square so that Members could park their cars there…

…and the very next month workmen were back scrubbing the lines out after the population of the Island let the politicians know in no uncertain terms that they would have to park on the road like everybody else!

An most unusual diversion for people on the beach in St Aubin's Bay came in the summer of 1967 when this massive generator for the Jersey Electricity Company was unloaded from a tank landing craft and driven up La Haule slip.

The coal elevator at the premises of the Jersey Gas Light Company in 1940.

And here is one of the engines inside the Jersey Gas Light Company. Gas would soon be used to drive motor vehicles as petrol became scarce during the German occupation.

Jersey's first lady posties appointed in 1947. The postman was Joe Machon and the woman on the right was a Mrs Warland. Unfortunately the other lady postie has not been identified.

The bakery at Pontac Stores in 1911. The frozen attitudes of the bakers was because, as the picture was taken indoors, they had to stand very still for several seconds while the camera shutter was open.

A 'building' of scrap paper stored at Bellozanne in March 1940. The war effort encouraged people not to waste anything.

'Number please?' was a question we were all asked back in the 1960s. But how many of us realised the spaghetti-like complexity with which the telephone girls had to cope in order to connect us at the Central Exchange?

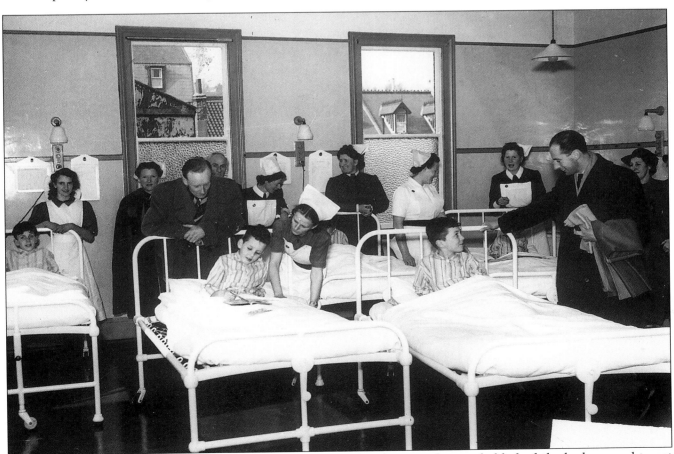

The children's ward at the General Hospital in the 1940s. The photographer probably had the beds moved to get everyone in the picture, otherwise the ward must have been pretty crowded!

After-school pleasures: There are ways and ways of flying a kite, but this has to be the ultimate in laid-back luxury in 1946!

Quite who is looking after whom is unclear, but what is certain is that this picture from a dog show at Springfield before the Occupation is a delight.

Timber, coffin boards and tree-felling are advertised on this Battle of Flowers float in the 1970s, as Marcel Bredonchel, John Hinault and Peter Hinault settle for a glass of Jersey cider to slake their thirst.

A lady golfer shows an admiring crowd of mainly men how to get out of a bunker at the Royal Jersey links at Grouville in the 1930s.

Physical training instructor Reg Nicolle demonstrates his strength and balance.

The popular Victoria College gym teacher also conducted open-air fitness classes for holidaymakers on the Lower Park in the late 1930s.

Personal fitness was very much the order of the day when a *News Chronicle* Instructor came to the Havre des Pas swimming pool in the 1930s and took classes for young…

…and the not quite-so-young.

Schoolchildren in the open stand at Springfield for the Island schools' annual sports meeting for the Cope Shield in May 1940, just a few weeks before the German occupation.

Twelve-year-old John Riley and 77-year-old J. Jerrom were probably the youngest and oldest starters ever at a point-to-point in Britain, when this picture was taken in January 1938. The young man sporting such a stylish cap was later to become Seigneur of Trinity and a prominent Island politician.

The Battle of Flowers in 1909 when horse-drawn floats were the order of the day. There was more than just strewn flowers to be cleaned up after the parade in those days!

Rule No 1 if you are a 'big-head' in the Battle of Flowers is to look where you're going and keep on your feet! This poor unfortunate fellow needed help to get him and his huge costume back into the vertical when he fell in the 1960s.

Dressed for the occasion. Two cricket teams in front of the old wooden pavilion at Victoria College Field at the beginning of the century, sporting a splendid range of headgear and blazers.

In the 1950s the British Chancellor allowed rebates on tax for those who married in the spring. This led to some Jersey hotels being filled with no guests other than honeymooners. Here some of the newly-weds are about to set out on a 'Honeymoon Special' outing with Mascot Coaches in 1956.

This picture is not actually as old as it looks, for it shows members of the Royal Jersey Agricultural and Horticultural Society in period costume for their 150th anniversary celebrations at Rosel Manor in 1983.

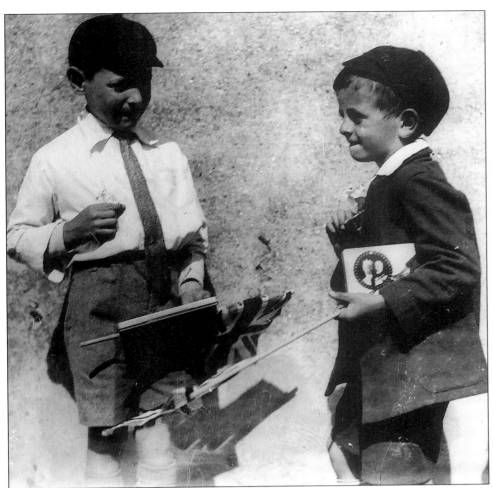

Two young schoolboys with their flags and boxes of presentation chocolates to mark the Silver Jubilee in 1935 of King George V and Queen Mary.

A study in concentration: Boys play with their model rowing boats at West Park swimming pool at the beginning of the century.

Fun in two of Jersey's rare snowfalls in 1947…

… and in 1958 when the dog decided to join in as well!

Little Barbara Lenton is carried around the ballroom as 'The Spirit of the New Year 1937' at the New Year Ball at West Park Pavilion.

Compared with the giant computerised fairground rides of today, these little swingboats may seem tame, but for these youngsters in the late 1940s they were just the ticket.

Hotel beach sports, and in particular the three-legged races, proved popular with contestants in St Ouen's Bay in the 1950s and '60s.

What greater fun can there be than trying to eat a Jersey wonder suspended on a string? None, apparently, judging by the looks of sheer pleasure on the faces of these Beeches boys at a fête in July 1938.

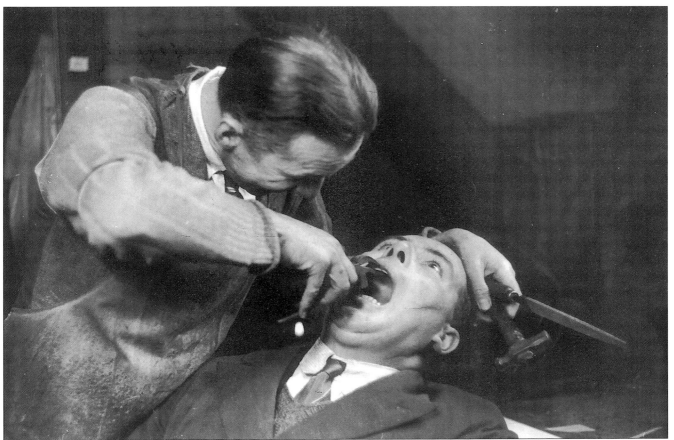

No this really isn't as bad as it looks, for it is two *Evening Post* employees, chief photographer Joss Higginbotham and proof reader Bruce Humber, fooling about when Joss had a bit of film left in his camera in 1939!

A children's party outside the Hotel de la Plage at Havre des Pas in the early 1950s, with the kiddies being entertained by a ventriloquist who smoked at the same time. Made a change from drinking a glass of water!

These delightful little schoolgirls at the Coronation 'Pageant of Progress' in May 1937 have their streamer flags to wave. On the left is Emily, the one in the middle was Pauline Balcam, and on the far right is Marie.

This monster pumpkin was photographed in 1937 at the St Clement's Show, but who grew it and who the little lad was is not recorded.

A family picnic just after the Occupation, but no further details are known.

A Christmas party at the General Hospital in 1932.

The splendid obelisk in Broad Street, St Helier, pictured here in 1898, is still there, but Barnes Boarding House and the Richmond English Boarding House are long gone.

View of Bouley Bay at the turn of the century. It shows the hillside devoid of trees but with follies of the Rockmount estate clearly visible on the skyline. Today the cliff side on the right of the jetty is heavily shored up.

Noel and Porter, the magnificent Victorian building which Linscott's once faced, was demolished in the late 1960s to make way for the BHS building.

Affectionately known as Jersey's Eiffel Tower, this 180-ft high structure, built in 1893, once towered over the St Louis Observatory. Sadly, it eventually became unsafe and had to be taken down in 1929.

The same tower in relation to the Institution Notre Dame de Bon Secours, a theological college. The building is now Highlands College.

The Promenade and railway line outside the Olympia Winter Garden and Grand Hotel, St Helier, at the turn of the century. The former was the venue for skating, circuses and many a splendid show.

La Rocco Tower in St Ouen's Bay in 1962, showing the damage done by the Germans who used it for target practice during the Occupation. It was repaired and restored in 1968 after a public appeal spearheaded by the Rev Peter Manton, later a senator.

Valley Farm, Queen's Valley, in the snow. The buildings are no longer visible since the valley was flooded at the end of the 1980s to form a reservoir. The outside of the farmhouses featured as Bergerac's home in the TV series.

The last town pump in St Helier, still to be seen in Francis Street, and around which many a good gossipy tale must have been told over the years.

In 1963 Linscotts of King Street looked out on to a road, and across it was the old Jersey firm of Noel and Porter.

Bunting and flags adorned King Street to celebrate the royal visit of King George V in 1921.

Pigeons roost and leave their signature behind. The Fire Brigade lends a hand in 1964 as deterrent sticky gunge is applied to the ledges of the States Building in a futile attempt to keep the birds at bay.

Charing Cross, St Helier, decorated with bunting and streamers for the Royal visit in 1957.

A double dose of Mary Ann nostalgia: Two pubs which no longer exist because they have been demolished to make way for modern buildings. The British Trinity (top), where the entrance to the Howard Davis Farm now stands; and (below) the old Union Inn on St John's Main Road, which Ann Street Brewery have replaced with a more modern roadhouse.

Havre des Pas at the turn of the century showing the promenade and the walkway 'bridge' to the Bathing Pool which orginally was intended to be for 'Ladies Bathing Only'.

The Royal Parade in 1903 showing the Don Monument unveiled 18 years before. While some of the splendid trees remain, those on the right of the picture are long gone.

Charing Cross in the 1920s, with Rutland Motor and Cycle Works in what is now a traffic-free precinct.

This photograph was taken in the 1920s in Bath Street and shows the granite sets in the roadway. The only easily identifiable landmark is the spire of St Mark's Church in the distance.

Two views of St Brelade's Bay taken in the 1960s. The promenade and beach remain the same, though there are many changes to the adjoining properties.

Queen Street, St Helier, around the turn of the century. Note the window on the right devoted entirely to Cadbury's products.

The Opera House, Gloucester Street, when it was both a theatre and a cinema. The billboard advertises 'The Man Who Knew Too Much', a film by Alfred Hitchcock made in 1933 and remade in 1956. This billing is for the latter. The theatre itself was undergoing restoration as the 20th century came to a close.

The Beresford Street Market in June 1936 before the adjoining Telephone Exchange was extended into it in the 1950s and the old fish market moved into the central area.

After the old fish market was demolished, the cattle market in Minden Place was used temporarily until the new fish market was completed.

Fire gutted the top storey of the Hotel de France in March 1994.

This was the railway level crossing at First Tower and in the distance can be seen the water tower on top of First Tower itself. Installed by the Jersey Waterworks Company in the 1890s, the huge tower and its weight of water cracked the round tower below, and it was removed in 1926.

Copp's kiln at Mont à l'Abbé was the last brick kiln in Jersey and a much-loved landmark. It was demolished in 1963 to make way for modern development.

The development or otherwise of Havre des Pas has been a contentious issue for some time now, but between the wars all that was required was a gentle stroll along the promenade while the youngsters played on the beach.

A cobbled Beresford Street, St Helier, around the turn of the century. The market building on the right has changed little, but the shop fronts on the left have now altered dramatically.

A magnificent panorama of the snow-covered Route du Fort and its environs in 1979, photographed from Fort Regent. The old Limes building on the right has now gone, to be replaced by modern nursing-care accommodation.

The annual pilgrimage to the Hermitage, where St Helier lived, on Elizabeth Castle. The procession pictured walking out along the causeway from West Park includes the Constable of St Helier in the 1970s, Peter Baker.

The extraordinary Princes Tower was built atop the chapels of La Hougue Bie in 1759. It was a popular tourist attraction until demolition was necessary in 1924 because the tower was unsafe.

Probably one of Jersey's most photographed and timeless scenes — the view from inside a cave at Plémont on the north coast.

Briggs and Company, whose Father Christmas grotto was legendary among Jersey children, dressed overall for the Coronation of George VI and Queen Elizabeth on 12 May 1937.

Queen Street in June 1955, when cars used the road and shoppers took their lives in their hands crossing from one side to the other.

Pier Road when it still had some of the old merchants' houses standing in 1971.

Grève de Lecq in Victorian times. Note the camera obscura, the small round building in the centre, from which the viewer could get a 360-degree panorama of the bay.

St Ouen's Bay under a lowering sky, with La Rocco Tower and Corbière Lighthouse almost in line.

The promenade opposite Gloucester Street, which was separated from the road by the railway. Note the rail car on the railway track, a very modern form of rail transport in 1925. This area of beach is now reclaimed and the Underpass runs through it.

King Street in January 1965. Note the way the traffic fills the street, making life difficult for shoppers — a problem solved when it became a pedestrian precinct in 1973.

Riding the cliff paths above Giffard Bay on the north coast in 1972, a spectacular if sometimes risky ride.

The magnificent façade of Trinity Manor which was build on the lines of a French château. The picture was taken during a Trinity parish garden fête in the 1960s.

Sand racing in St Ouen's Bay has long been a great spectator sport for Islanders, as can be seen from this splendid photograph of the Grand Prix race in September 1936.

This Jersey New Waterworks Company van attracted a large crowd after it turned turtle in St Helier in the early 1950s.

The bus is not quite what it seems, for it is not delivering passengers to the de Havilland biplane on West Park beach in 1936 when that was Jersey's only air strip. It was the airline's booking office, and the fares are displayed on the roof rack edge.

Jersey once had several bus companies, and the Jersey Bus Service, better known as Joe's Bus Services, run by Joe Manning, was the last small private company before the JMT took over. In 1958 this JBS bus was advertising the facts that cooking by electricity was cheaper and cleaner, and that Ovaltine was the world's best nightcap!

This impressive-looking set up is actually the St Brelade fire engine from 1900 — though the fire hose looks as though it may have had more holes in it than just the one at the end!

This double-decker, which came to Jersey as No 12 in the JMT fleet in May 1959, was taken out of service in October 1973. In April 1974 it was given this sunshine livery and sent to the Sisters of the Immaculate Conception at St Méen Le Grand in Brittany to be used to transport under-privileged children of Paris on holiday.

It's farewell to this No 16 double-decker as it is placed in the slings for transportation out of the Island…

…to be loaded on to the mv *Nincop*. The Island's double-deckers left the Island for good in February 1971.

Petrol was at a premium during the war years, so what better way to power your car than with coal gas? All it required was a very large gas bag on the top! The proud driver was Alf Britton.

Mobility is the keynote for this St John Ambulance man on duty in St Ouen's Bay at the sand racing in July 1956. His Lee Enfield is a fine example of British engineering and would be worth a small fortune today.

This mobile electricity show room was something of a sensation in February 1955 as it travelled around the Island. Here it is parked in Vine Street alongside the Royal Square.

A fine shot of two racing cars abreast along the Inner Road during the international road races around the West Park to Bel Royal circuit in the late 1940s.

There was never any chance of this motor car winning any beauty prizes. It was a Bond, made by Sharps Commercials of Preston, Lancashire, in 1948 and '49. It had a two-stroke Villiers engine and a three-speed motorcycle gear system. On one occasion in St Helier the brake cable snapped and bowled a policeman on point duty over — but fortunately only the pride of driver and bobby were hurt.

Crowds of passengers disembark after the mailboat berths at the Albert Pier in July 1946.

A tragic place crash at Corbière in August 1970 when this Beagle ploughed into a garden shed and the pilot, Ken Desmond, was killed. Mr Desmond was the personal pilot of Leonard Matchan the millionaire industrialist and owner of Brecqhou.

Deep snow at Jersey Airport in the bitter winter of 1958, an event so rare that the only available way to clear the forecourt was by shovel and good old-fashioned elbow grease!

Before the new airport roads were built, this lane across the end of the airfield meant that car drivers had to take their lives in their hands, so a simple red light and a notice were installed to prevent two wings and four wheels inadvertently meeting.

Because of the danger to the very heavy air traffic in and out of Jersey, gliding is no longer allowed, but in the 1930s the Jersey Gliding Club's craft could be seen regularly taking to the air at St Ouen.

The autogyro was an extraordinary aircraft — a cross between a plane and a helicopter, of which it was the prototype. It was powered by a propeller at the front, and as the craft moved forward the top propeller, which had no power, began to revolve with wind pressure, providing the lift as conventional wings would have done. This example landed in Jersey, both in a field and on the beach, in 1933, showing Islanders the latest miracle of flight.

This intriguing picture shows a Dakota of Air Transport Charter Channel Islands parked on the apron at Nairobi's (Eastleigh) Airport in the mid-1940s. The aircraft was piloted by Capt K.M. Gosling and it had a short but very full life. Built in 1943 it was bought by Air Charter in 1947 and flew cattle and people to and from Africa and India. It crashed in 1951 at Manchester, ploughing into a greenhouse while carrying newspapers, but no one was hurt.

The Jersey coastline stretches below the incoming British European Airways de Havilland Heron, G-ALZL. The aircraft was a familiar sight in the skies above the Island in the 1950s.

Firemen and airport officials gather up instruments and appliances from the air crash in 1938 when 17 people, including a baby, lost their lives. One was a farmworker who had been in the field where the plane crashed.

The light aircraft taking part in the Jersey International Air Rally in May 1955 neatly lined up behind the old airport buildings.

Jersey Airport in 1951 with a de Havilland Heron, G-ALZL, of British European Airways parked on the apron.

The very modern and up-to-date radio installation at Jersey Airport in February 1938 was used to contact with UK airports for advice and information on when aircraft were on their way to the Island.

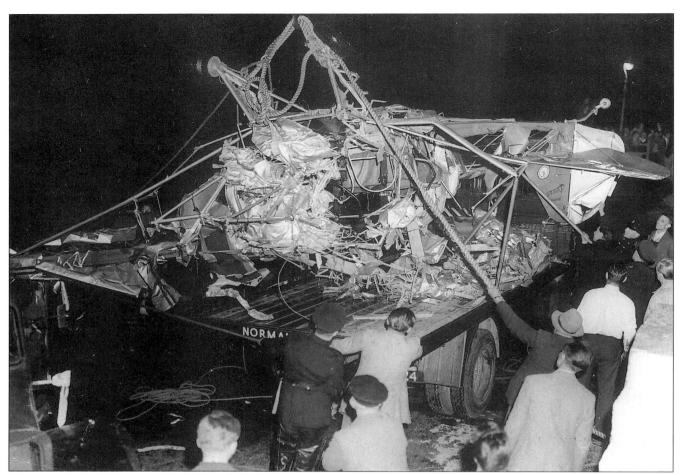

The mangled wreckage of an Auster aircraft which plunged into the sea off Gorey after the air rally in 1959. Three people lost their lives in the accident.

A impressive cavalcade of motor buses outside the Terminus Hotel, St Aubin, in the early 1930s, advertising 'Most comfortable buses and through fares from St Helier's Station'. The building is now St Brelade's Parish Hall.

This aircraft being manhandled along Gloucester Street landed on the beach at West Park in the 1930s and had to be brought up into town to be refuelled at Stevenson's Garage.

The St Aubin's Bay, a de Havilland 84 biplane, on West Park Beach in the summer of 1935.

Jersey Airport when it first opened in 1937. The buildings in the foreground are St Peter's Barracks and Holiday Camp.

And the same Airport in 1967. All the planes on the apron are Dakotas, and the curving Airport Road has not yet been replaced by L'Avenue de la Reine Elizabeth II.

This picture of a Jersey family in a carriage was taken in Waterworks Valley around 1914.

These two boys in blue are not waiting to arrest someone on West Park beach. They are on duty at what was Jersey's only air strip in the 1930s, when de Havilland aircraft, like the Giffard Bay pictured here, landed and took off among the sunbathers.

A cavalcade of magnificent motor cars drive around the statue of Queen Victoria when it stood at the Weighbridge, where the bus station now is, at the turn of the century.

A rare sea visit by the British Air Minister, the Rt Hon Sir Samuel Hoare, in 1928, ended with his departure on this magnificent new all-metal Short seaplane, one the largest aircraft of its time. He is seen taking leave of the Lieut-Governor, Major General Sir Francis Bingham, raising his hat, and the Bailiff, Sir William Vernon, seated.

Royal Visitors

The Prince of Wales, the future King Edward VIII, visiting Victoria College to open the Howard Davis Hall in July 1935.

King George V and Queen Mary entering the States Building during their visit in 1921.

The Queen Mother talking to Miss Lilian Le Couteur during her visit in 1984.

If you want to meet royalty then get a hat — a fine display of millinery during the visit of the Queen Mother in 1963.

Jersey welcomed Queen Elizabeth, now the Queen Mother, and King George VI in 1946, soon after Liberation. This was the first visit by a reigning monarch since 1921.

The young Prince Charles as a student at Oxford University, digging for archaeological treasure in the cave at La Cotte, Ouaisnê, in March 1968.

Princess Anne, now the Princess Royal, shows how to wear a hat with style on her visit in 1972.

The then Seigneur of Trinity, Major John Riley, presents the traditional pair of mallards on a silver platter as an act of fealty to Queen Elizabeth in the Royal Court in June 1978.

Marina, Duchess of Kent, receiving a salute outside the States Building in 1949.

Prince Edward receives a welcoming address from the Lieut-Governor, Admiral Sir William Pillar, in July 1986.

Watched by Prince Philip and the Bailiff, Sir Alexander Coutanche, Princess Elizabeth receives a bouquet from a young Brownie in the Howard Davis Park during their visit in 1949…

… and meets the nurses who are all wearing white gloves — for shaking the royal hand perhaps?

Princess Anne shakes hands with David Bellamy, while Sir Yehudi Menuhin and Jeremy Taylor look on, at a charity concert in October 1984.

Princess Margaret is introduced to the Constable of St Helier, Peter Baker, by the Bailiff, Sir Frank Ereaut, in October 1977. In the centre of the picture is Solicitor-General Philip Bailhache who was to become Bailiff in 1995.

The Queen and the Duke of Edinburgh in the Great Hall at Victoria College in 1957. The Queen is receiving the loyal address from head boy Richard Le Brocq.

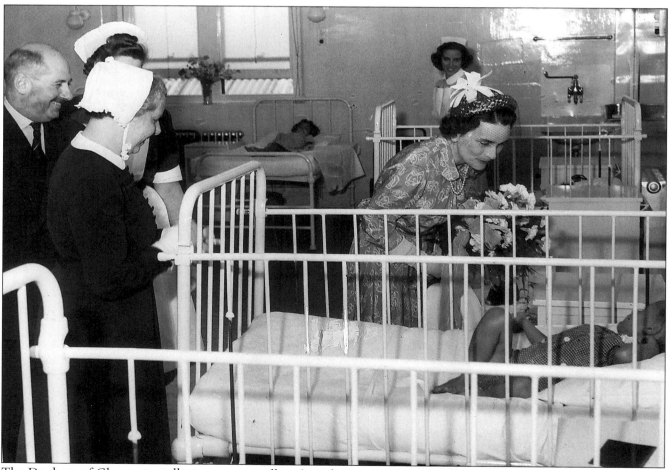

The Duchess of Gloucester talks to a very small patient during a visit to the General Hospital in 1952.

Cheering crowds lined the roads of the country parishes to catch a glimpse of Her Majesty Queen Elizabeth II and Prince Philip when they visited the Island in 1957.

On the same visit Prince Philip 'goes walkabout'.

A picture which recalls happier days for a royal couple who visited the Island in 1987. The Duke and Duchess of York came to Jersey that year to celebrate the airport's 50th anniversary.

A delightful portrait of Princess Margaret as she leaves Jersey aboard a plane of the Queen's Flight after her visit in June 1952…

…during which she attended a grand gala ball in aid of charity. With Her Royal Highness is the Bailiff, Mr Cecil Harrison.

The Duchess of Kent arrives at Jersey Airport by helicopter in May 1985 to be greeted by the Lieut-Governor, Admiral Sir William Pillar.

Three cheers for Queen Elizabeth the Queen Mother when she visits the Island in 1984 to launch a lifeboat appeal.

The Queen Mother inspects lifeboat crew under the watchful eye of Harbourmaster Capt Roy Bullen…

…and shows a delightful touch of informality when a young man at Maufant Youth Centre invites her to take his shot at pool — which she does with consummate skill.

Princess Margaret walks across a farm field in 1959 accompanied by young farmer John Le Gallais, later a Deputy in the States of Jersey.

Marina, Duchess of Kent, receives a welcoming address at the Hospital when she opens the Nurses' Home in July 1948 …

...and a generation later the new Duchess of Kent has the 'V' inscription in the paving of the Royal Square explained to her by the Bailiff, Sir Frank Ereaut, as stonemason Maurice Le Guyader and his son David look on. The 'V' was incorporated into repair work by Mr Le Guyader — working under the noses of the occupying forces in 1944 — and marked both the life-saving arrival of the Red Cross ship *Vega* and the impending Allied victory.

The Queen delights in the company of the children of Le Squez School during her visit in 1989.

The Duke and Duchess of Gloucester pose in the doorway of the States Building on their official visit in July 1952...

...while in 1978 the next generation Duke and Duchess of Gloucester are shown the Royal Mace by the Bailiff, Sir Frank Ereaut.

Marina, Duchess of Kent, framed in an archway at Mont Orgueil Castle, during her visit in August 1949 with her children, Alexandra and Michael.

Princess Elizabeth and Prince Philip flank the Bailiff, Sir Alexander Coutanche, during their visit in 1949.